design focus Product

G7

G7组合的产品设计

关于 G7

三十年来，欧洲设计作品大量涌入美国，对美国设计师构成威胁。美国设计师所受的教育把意大利式设计视为权威，对意式设计所体现出来的民族精神满怀敬畏。这种气氛下熏陶出来的美国设计者们要最终摆脱这种束缚的确需要很大的勇气。尽管二战后美国的偶像如埃姆斯、诺尔和赫尔曼·米勒的影响仍然很大，但近几年来，似乎越来越有必要对美国的设计重新定义。

一九九五年，一家名为"TOTEM 设计"的艺廊（或者说是商店）在纽约的 TRIBECA 区开业。TOTEM 意在为那些期望找到恰当的制造及销售场所的设计师提供帮助。

G7 是一个联合展，由以下成员构成：博姆设计公司的皮尔·博格纳，CCD 设计公司的克里斯托弗·迪姆，柯玛设计公司的大卫·库力与罗伯托·古兹曼，迪纳森设计公司的迈克尔·索里斯和尼克·戴恩，样板制作公司的罗斯·梅纽兹和克里斯·邦迪，以及恩斯组合的玛利·莫尔里，哈利·鲍尔·凡·伊尔塞和卡米拉·维加。G7 是双关语，也有七大工业国之意。

G7 联展组织这一设想是由 TOTEM 的创办董事大卫·希勒提出的，此后 G7 就在其成员设计师的热忱努力下逐渐成长起来。在过去的三年里，G7 在纽约、巴黎和米兰举办的国际家具博览会上组织了数次展览，这些展览是由 TOTEM 和时尚流行杂志《SURFACE》共同承办与赞助。这些活动有助于在国际媒体上建立起美式家具及家居办公用品的地位。

TOTEM 和 G7 之间的关系并不简单。实际上，TOTEM 想创建一个品牌（G7），并想通过 G7 联展在国际上成功树立艺廊形象。在颇受欢迎的活动上展出的展品已经成为一种系统的街道景观，吸引了美国迅猛增长的电子经济的新老消费者。TOTEM 的力量就在于它依靠着年轻的一代城市消费者，他们富有且具品味。TOTEM 的季刊《DSGN》也是其所售商品的重要宣传渠道。《DSGN》同时还充当内行设计生活方式的推广工具。然而，展览终归是一种短期的形式，它在短期内引起的公众效应并不一定能帮助家具生产筹集资金。TOTEM 已被看成是与 G7 联展同出一体，而不用冒险购买展品。也许 TOTEM 和 G7 关系的复杂性在于 TOTEM 总想同时担任多种角色，先是作为一家艺廊商店开业，从事小规模的制作及出版刊物。现在希勒正计划在苏豪区开一家新的艺廊，有别于 TRIBECA 的原艺廊。这可能会划清各个场所各自的角色。新的艺廊专门从事设计实验品的展出，而原来的商店则主要出售各种制作成品。

虽然 TOTEM 已经成功地建立起一个涵盖创作人、生产商和销售商的网络，G7 有可能最终无法确定自己的形式。当 G7 众多成员都面临着各类国际性的事务时，G7 联展会发生什么变化呢？它还会是个每年举办展览会的非正式组织吗？或者因为成员设计者太忙碌而最终解散，或者 G7 会继续发展下去，比如作为一种商业行为而筹资？他们会找到一个独立的生产商来赞助他们的项目吗？我们是否要再等一年呢？

In the past 30 years American designers have been inundated and often intimidated by European design imports. Educated in the absolute awe for Italian design manufacturing structures and products, and their ability to embody the spirit of a nation, it took Americans some guts to finally cut the cord. Lately it looks like there has been a strong impetus to redefine the identity of American design, long after the still overpowering presence of post-war American icons such as the Eames, and other Knoll and Herman Miller's protégés.

Totem Design opened in New York in 1995 as a gallery/store in Tribeca with the intent to promote American modern designers, those desperate to find the proper venues for manufacturing and distribution.

G7 is an exhibition group composed of the following members: Pierre Bouguennec of Boum Design; Christopher C. Deam of CCD; David Khouri and Roberto Guzman of Comma; Michael Solis and Nick Dine of Dinersan; Ross Menuez and Chris Bundy of Prototype and Production and Marre Moerel, Harry Paul van Iersel and Camila Vega of Once Group.

The name G7 is a pun taken on the international geopolitics meetings of the top 7 most powerful countries in the world.

The group has grown organically and spontaneously under the impulse of each enthusiastic participating designer, while having been created as a concept by David Shearer, founding director of Totem. Over the past three years a number of exhibitions have been organized during the international furniture fairs in New York, Paris and Milan: they were curated and co-sponsored by Totem and the trendy fashion magazine Surface. These events have helped identify in the international press an American trend in furniture, home and office accessories.

The relationships between Totem and G7 are complex. Totem has actually managed to build a brand (the G7) and has cultivated the store's image largely on the international success of the group. The works shown during these popular social gatherings, which have systematically turned into a street phenomenon, attract the hip and youngster buyers of the booming American "e-conomy". The strength of Totem is to have built on this younger generation of sophisticated, urban and wealthy consumers. Totem's quarterly magazine DSGN has also been a significant advertising channel for the pieces for sale in the store, and also a vehicle to promulgate a hip design lifestyle. But an exhibition remains an ephemeral event, which beyond the immediate glitzy publicity effect does not necessarily finances the manufacturing of the furniture which often remains a limited edition or at a prototype stage. Totem has been identified with the names of G7 talents without always taking the risk of purchasing the pieces in exhibit. Perhaps the complexity of the relationship is due to the fact that Totem has attempted to play more than one role at a time. Totem started as a store+gallery aside from undertaking small-scale manufacturing and publishing projects. Now that Shearer is planning to open a new gallery space in Soho, separate from the original Tribeca space, it will probably clarify the missions of each venue. The new gallery will be completely devoted to showcasing design experiments. The store will focus on selling manufactured pieces.

Although Totem has succeeded in creating a unique place and an interface between creators, manufacturing and distribution networks, G7 may not have found its final form yet. What will happen with G7 when lots of his members have embraced international careers? Will it stay as an informal group putting up exhibitions once a year, will it dissolve due to the busy schedule and agenda of each of the member designers, or will it move to the next step, i.e. to get incorporated and financed as a business? Could they find one single manufacturer to finance their projects? Shall we wait next year?

Laetitia Wolff, May 2000

第二届 G7 家具年展

独到的设计和"现代气息"的体现一定出自欧洲设计师和厂家之手，这一观念正受到 TOTEM、《SURFACE》杂志和"孟买蓝宝石"的联合挑战，其中 TOTEM 是纽约现代设计的领先展场。由七间美国新秀公司组成的 G7 刚刚结束在米兰 2000 国际家具博览会的展览，现正在纽约举办的国际现代家具博览会上第二次展示他们最新的作品。

把多样化的设计范例推介到一个大型博览会，G7 在老套的家具与工业设计产品中抢尽风头。去年的 G7 展引起了来自国际时尚出版物的强烈反响，也标志着新一代美国消费者的实力。

G7 是一个拥有获奖天才的组合集团，其中包括期待着在美国追寻艺术和商业的融合的外国移民。在这里，人们可以看到荷兰智利的三人组合恩斯（玛利·莫尔里，哈利·鲍尔·凡·伊尔塞和卡米拉·维加）的作品体现的生态主题；总部设在旧金山的 CCD 设计公司（克里斯托弗·迪姆）作品所体现的"少即多"的精神；法国博姆设计公司（皮尔·博格纳）自我教诲精神所表现出来的"了解－行动－工艺"的形式；样板制作公司（罗斯·梅纽兹和克里斯·邦迪）的冷静态度；渥克斯公司（迈克尔·索里斯）深受科幻小说影响而采用的未来几何图形；柯玛设计公司（大卫·库力和罗伯托·古兹曼）简化而多功能的家具；以及迪纳森设计公司（尼可·戴恩）功利而时尚的设计。

G7 不但拥有运动员般的竞争意识，它的自发性与不断的创新让其充满活力。G7 的组成就是为了进入曾一度遭到冷落的休闲设计时代。G7 的设计不仅线条优美，功能齐全，而且变化无常及幽默。在它的展会上，处处都是外型线条性感，用材独特，有背叛意识的展品。

TOTEM 的创建人大卫·希勒认为 G7 代表了一场真正的美国设计运动的开端，这是一场我们在过去三四十年来曾看过的运动。"看到几年来一直受到熏陶的设计师终于得到了应有的承认，真有说不出的欣慰"。

现代艺术博物馆的建筑与设计馆馆长鲍拉·安东尼也赞同希勒的感慨："现在新一代的美国设计者已经走在最前沿，很快他们将会打破创新的平衡格局。纽约拥有大量的艺术家、室内与平面设计师、建筑师、艺术指导和多媒体设计师，今天它终于又以同样的热情欢迎家具设计师、产品设计师。这是美国设计的伟大时刻。"

Totem, New York's leading showcase for contemporary design, has teamed up with Surface Magazine and Bombay Sapphire to challenge the notion that good design and the meaning of "modern" must necessarily be dictated by European designers and manufacturers. Coming straight from an off-site showing during the Salone Internationale del Mobile in Milan 2000, G7, comprised of seven American upstarts, now present their latest work together for a second time during the ICFF (International Contemporary Furniture Fair) in New York.

Offering an alternative design paradigm to the one dominant at the large fairs, G7 proposes to steal some thunder away from the old standards in furniture and industrial design. Last year's G7 event garnered an enthusiastic response from the international lifestyle press, validating the power of a sophisticated new American consumer.

G7 is a varied group of award-winning proteges and prodigies - including immigrants eager to chase the fusion of art and commerce in the United States. Visitors can see the biological theme in the works of Dutch-Chilean trio Once (Marre Moerrel, Harry Paul Van Iersel and Camila Vega); the less-is-more ethos of San Francisco-based CCD (Christopher C. Deam); the savoir-faire-technological forms of French auto-didactic Pierre Bouguennec's Boum Design; the cool-headed approach of Prototype & Production (Chris Bundy and Ross Menuez); the science-fiction inspired, near-future geometric shapes of Worx (Michael Solis); the reductionist and multi-functional furniture of Comma (David Khouri and Roberto Guzman); and the utilitarian chic designs of Dinersan, Inc. (Nick Dine).

Besides a sportsmanlike spirit of competition, G7 is fueled by elements of spontaneity and surprise. Built with the intention to deflate the solitude of the chat-room era, these designs are built with as much levity and humor as they are streamlined for form and function. Sexy lines, unlikely materials and renegade constructions will fill the exhibition space.

Totem's founder David Shearer believes that G7 represents the beginning of a true American design movement, the likes of which we haven't seen for the past thirty or forty years. "It's incredibly rewarding to see the designers we've been nurturing for several years finally getting the recognition that they deserve."

Paola Antonelli, curator of architecture and design at the MoMA, echoes Shearer's sentiments. "A new generation of American designers has recently come the forefront and will soon move the balance of creativity toward this side of the world," she said. "New York has at last embraced furniture and product design with the same proud passion with which it has celebrated its own local artists, interior and graphic designers, architects, art directors and multimedia mavericks. It is a great moment for American design".

David Shearer,
Founding director of Totem
New York, May 2000

皮尔·博格纳／博姆设计公司

皮尔·博格纳来自法国布列塔克。一九八七年抵达纽约。以其在建筑与柜子制作的自学背景，他于一九八九年开设博姆设计公司。博姆设计公司将机敏处事的才能与新技术结合，一直致力采用普列克斯玻璃与聚氯乙烯材料制作系列组合家具。博格纳正为纽约、迈阿密与长岛的住宅项目进行设计。

PIERRE BOUGUENNEC/ BOUM DESIGN

Hailing from Brittany, France, Pierre Bouguennec landed in New York in 1987. With an auto-didactic background in architecture and cabinet making, he founded Boum Design in 1989. Combining age-old savoir faire with new technology, Boum has been hard at work on a series of modular spaces crafted from plexiglass and inflatable PVC. Bouguennec also has residential projects underway in New York, Miami and Long Island.

P6 位于纽约 TRIBECA 区弗郎克林街的 TOTEM 艺廊

P6 Totem gallery in New York Tribeca area, on Franklin Street

P12-14 组合 1. 1990

P12-14 Unit One, 1990

P12-14 设计: 皮尔·博格纳

P12-14 Design: Pierre Bouguennec

P34 电插座，1997
制造：里格勒·罗瑟特
P34 Plug In, 1997
Manufacture: Ligne Roset

P34 设计：皮尔·博格纳
P34 Design: Pierre Bouguennec

P34 电插座，1997
制造：里格勒·罗瑟特
P34 Plug In, 1997
Manufacture: Ligne Roset

P34 设计：皮尔·博格纳

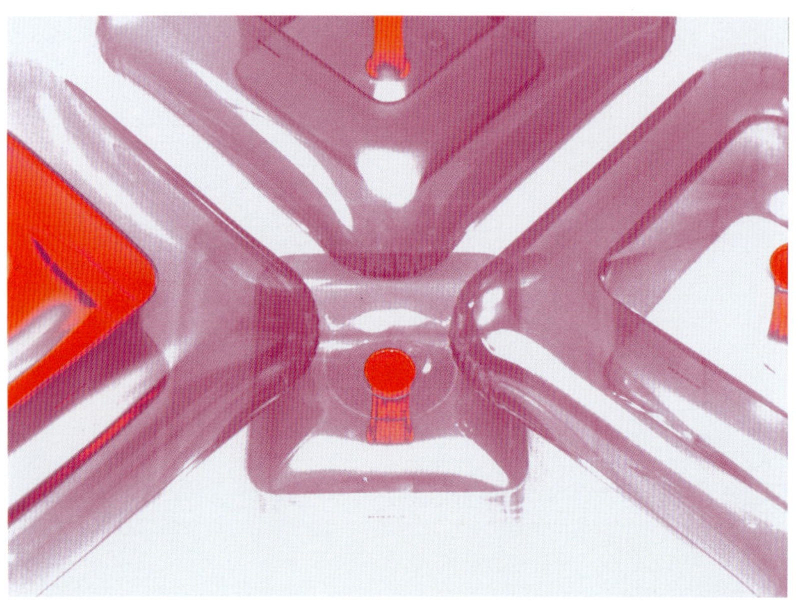

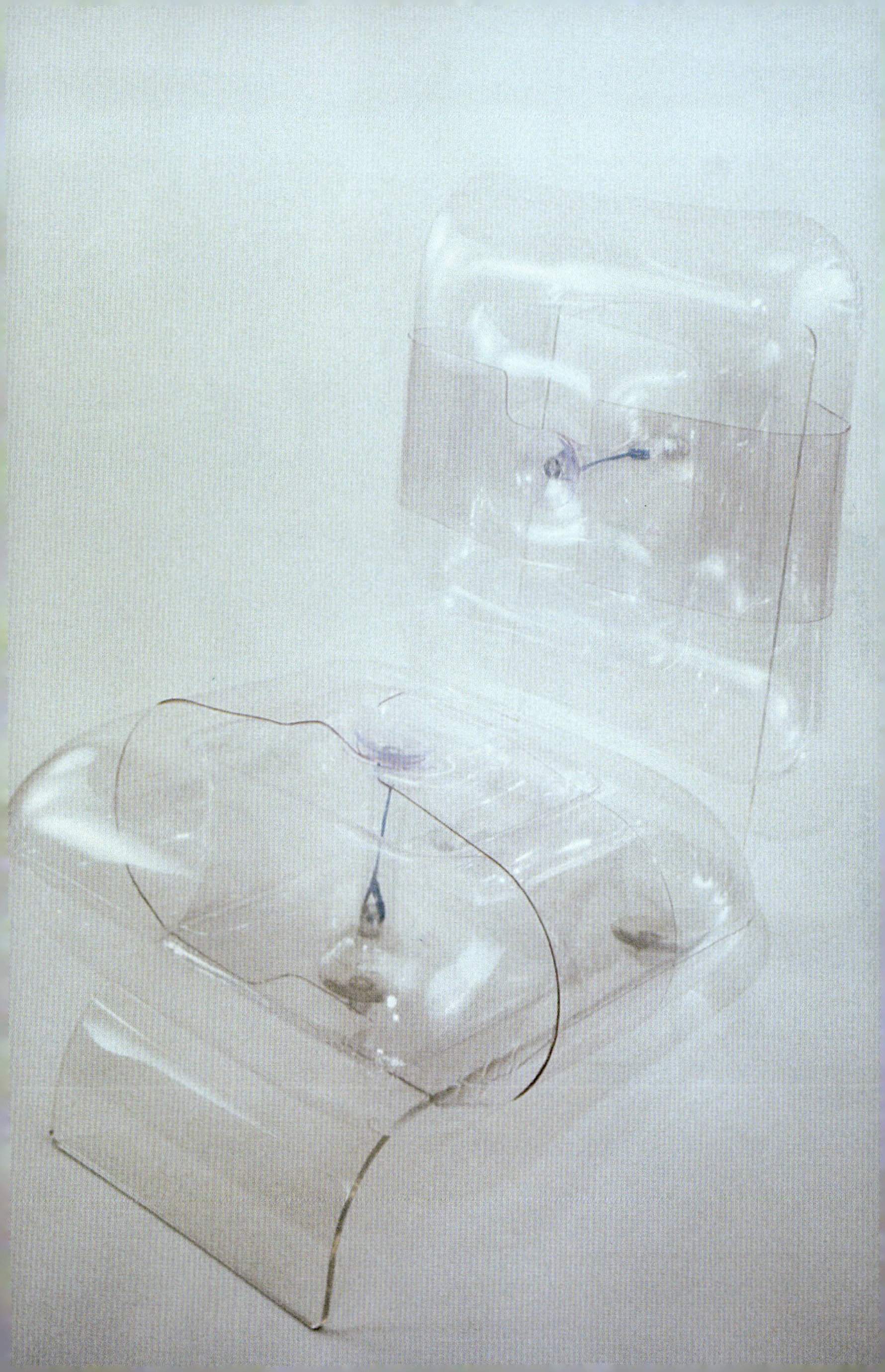

P36 "空气"系列（局部），1999-2000
材料：聚氯乙烯塑料
P36 Air series (detail), 1999-2000
Materials: PVC

P37 "空气"系列（屏风），1999-2000
材料：聚氯乙烯塑料
P37 Air series (screen), 1999-2000
Materials: PVC

P38 "空气"系列（彩色椅子），1999-2000
材料：聚氯乙烯塑料
P38 Air series (chair colored), 1999-2000
Materials: PVC

P39 "空气"系列（椅子），1999-2000
材料：聚氯乙烯塑料
P39 Air series (chair), 1999-2000
Materials: PVC

P40-41 "空气"系列（折叠式躺椅），1999-2000
材料：聚氯乙烯塑料
P40-41 Air series (unfolded lounge chair), 1999-2000
Materials: PVC

P42 "空气"系列（躺椅局部），1999-2000
材料：聚氯乙烯塑料
P42 Air series (lounge chair detail), 1999-2000
Materials: PVC

P36-42 设计：皮尔·博格纳
P36-42 Design: Pierre Bouguennec

P44-46　″空气″系列在纽约新康耐店展出
P44-46　Air Series exhibited at the new Conran Shop in New York

P44-46　设计：皮尔·博格纳
P44-46　Design: Pierre Bouguennec

大卫·库力与罗伯托·古兹曼／柯玛设计公司

大卫·库力与罗伯托·古兹曼于一九九七年在法拉迪龙区创办了柯玛设计公司，这个地区，几乎所有的家具都是当地生产的。

在一九九八年纽约国际现代家具博览会上，大卫·库力与罗伯托·古兹曼首次展出他们的十五件家具。

柯玛设计公司坚信家具和室内产品本身就应具有说服力，相关的说明应该越精简越好。关于这一问题，柯玛设计公司有几点感受颇深：首先，简洁是设计师面临的最大挑战。其次，他们致力将普通的材料以独特的方式巧妙运用。最后，他们期望创新，在一些陈旧的设计上赋予全新的形式，并使之容易使用及具多种功能。

目前柯玛设计公司主要由大卫·库力（总裁）和罗伯托·古兹曼（伙伴）构成。

大卫·库力是目前处于一线的设计师，他来自加利福尼亚，后迁到纽约就读于哥伦比亚大学研究生院。一九八七年，他获得建筑学和历史保护科学硕士双学位。之后一直在布恩伙伴公司工作，这是在苏豪区的一间小型建筑公司，直到一九九七年离开那里创办了柯玛设计公司。在布恩伙伴公司工作期间，他先是负责零售和展示设计项目，包括 HALSTON SIGNATURE 及位于麦迪逊大街的 KENAR 服装公司的旗舰商店，餐厅项目包括旧金山的 FARALLON 和纽约的 METRONOME，同时还有住宅项目。

凑巧的是，罗伯托·古兹曼也来自加利福尼亚，之后在哥伦比亚大学研究生院读书并获得建筑学硕士学位。自一九八七年毕业后，他就作为设计师为不同的公司工作，包括科恩、彼得森、霍士及彼得·马里奥伙伴公司。他同时作为助理艺术总监为以下的项目作场景设计：一九九六年夏季奥林匹克运动会，一九九七年格莱美颁奖典礼。以前做过的项目包括 VIACOM、MTV、VHI、NICKELODEON、位于 FOLEY 广场的联邦法院、RALPH LAUREN 及 POLO SPORT 等公司的室内设计。目前，他为伦敦的一个住宅项目做设计。

David Khouri and Roberto Guzman / COMMA

David Khouri and Roberto Guzman founded Comma in 1997 in the Flatiron District of where almost all of pieces are produced locally.

The 1998 International Contemporary Furniture Fair in New York constituted the first viewing of their initial fifteen pieces into the furniture market.

While firmly believing that furniture and interiors should speak for themselves and verbiage about them should be kept to a minimum, there are a few points about which Comma feels strongly. Firstly, they enjoy being seduced by the simple idea to discover that reducing anything to its most archetypal form is by far the biggest challenge to any designer. Secondly, they are dedicated to introducing pieces which manipulate familiar materials in unfamiliar ways, and lastly, they look forward to evolving, to presenting new pieces which grow out of the ideas originally stated, but take on wholly new forms, always remaining accessible and multi-functional.

Comma is presently made up of David Khouri, principal, and Roberto Guzman, partner. David Khouri is the designer of the current line. Originally from California, he moved to New York to attend graduate school at Columbia University, where, in 1987, he received both a Master of Architecture and a Master of Science in Historic Preservation. He worked as senior associate at Bohn Associates, a small Soho architectural firm until leaving in 1997 to begin Comma. While at Bohn Associates, he primarily designed retail and showroom projects, including Halston Signature and Kenar Clothing's Madison Avenue flagship store, as well as restaurants, including Farallon in San Francisco and Metronome in New York, as well as residences.

Roberto Guzman is from California as well and attended Columbia where he received a Master of Architecture degree. Since graduating in 1987, he has worked as a designer for various firms, including Kohn, Pederson, Fox and Peter Marino Associates. He has also worked in set design as an assistant art director for such projects as the 1996 Summer Olympics and the 1997 Grammy Awards. Past projects include corporate offices for Viacom, MTV, VH1 and Nickelodeon, the new U.S. Federal Courthouse at Foley Square, Ralph Lauren and Polo Sport. He is currently working on a residence in London.

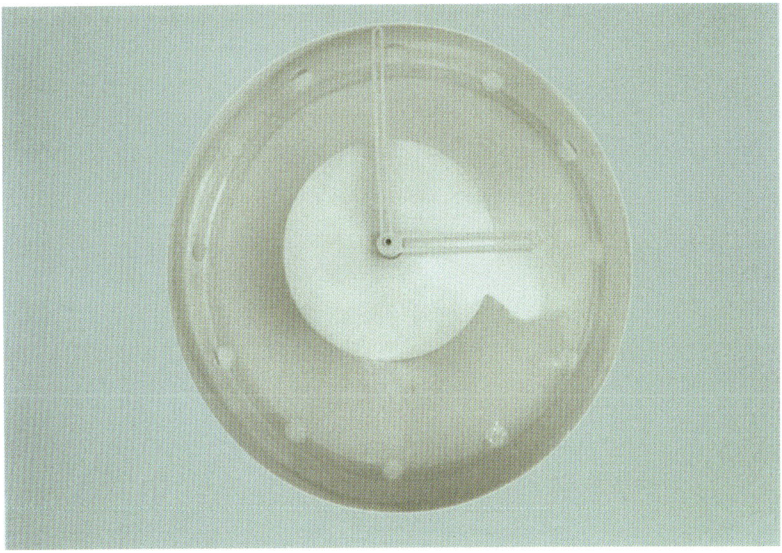

P50 折叠屏风 2. 1998-2000
材料: 塑料
P50 Screen 2, 1998-2000
Materials: lacquered acrylic

P52 LOVETH 躺椅, 1998-2000
材料: 皮革、不锈钢
P52 Loveth Lounge, 1998-2000
Materials: oxblood calfskin, stainless steel legs.
Also available in mohair.

P53 抽屉柜 19. 1998-2000
材料: 铝、胡桃木夹板
P53 Drawer Unit 19, 1998-2000
Materials: aluminum, walnut veneer oil finish &
white Corian top. Also available in East Indian
rosewood

P54 END 桌子 19. 1998-2000
材料: 铝、胡桃木夹板
P54 End Table 19, 1998-2000
Materials: aluminum, walnut veneer oil finish.
Also available in East Indian rosewood.

P55 DOOKIA 展示架, 1998-2000
材料: 乳白塑料架、钢座
P55 Dookia Display Unit, 1998-2000
Materials: milk acrylic shelves & powder coated
steel base.

P56-57 LOVEME 鸡尾酒桌, 1998-2000
材料: 东印度玫瑰木、不锈钢
P56-57 LoveMe Cocktail Table, 1998-2000
Materials: Mirror finished East Indian rosewood
top, stainless steel legs. Also available in
lacquer finish.

P58 ZELPHA 桌和 GORME 桌, 1998-2000
材料: 不锈钢板
P58 Zelpha Table and Gorme table, 1998-2000
Materials: 12 gauge stainless steel.

P59（上） VESPERS 蜡烛盒, 1998-2000
材料: 喷砂松木、胡桃木
P59 (Top) Vespers Candlebox, 1998-2000
Materials: Sand blasted cedar walnut stain.

P59（下） 柯玛钟. 1998-2000
材料: 圆玻璃钟面、金属指针、电池
P59 (Bottom) Clock, 1998-2000
Materials: 13" Diameter glass face, etched hour
markers and white metal hands battery.

P60-61 MARY JANE . 1998-2000
材料: 聚酯树脂、大理石、铝
P60-61 Mary Jane Console, 1998-2000
Materials: Polyesther resin, white carraba
marble top, aluminum base and legs

P62-63 LULU 墙灯. 1998-2000
材料: 丙烯酸塑料、电子开关板、绝缘吊板
P62-63 Lulu Lights, Wall lights, 1998-2000
Materials: Acrylic, electrified starter plate.
unelectrified suspended plates. Available in
several colors.

P64 VALET OF DOLLS 台
台面用于放钥匙、零钱、信、药丸及杂物.
1998-2000
材料: 聚酯树脂、丙烯酸塑料
P64 Valet of the Dolls Table, 1998-2000
Top is recessed for keys, change, letters, pills
and other pocket debris. Concealed light
source silhouettes objects.
Materials: Polyester resin & acrylic.

P50-61/P64 设计: 大卫 · 库力·
P50-61/P64 Design: David Khouri

P62-63 设计: 罗伯托 · 古兹曼
P62-63 Design: Roberto Guzman

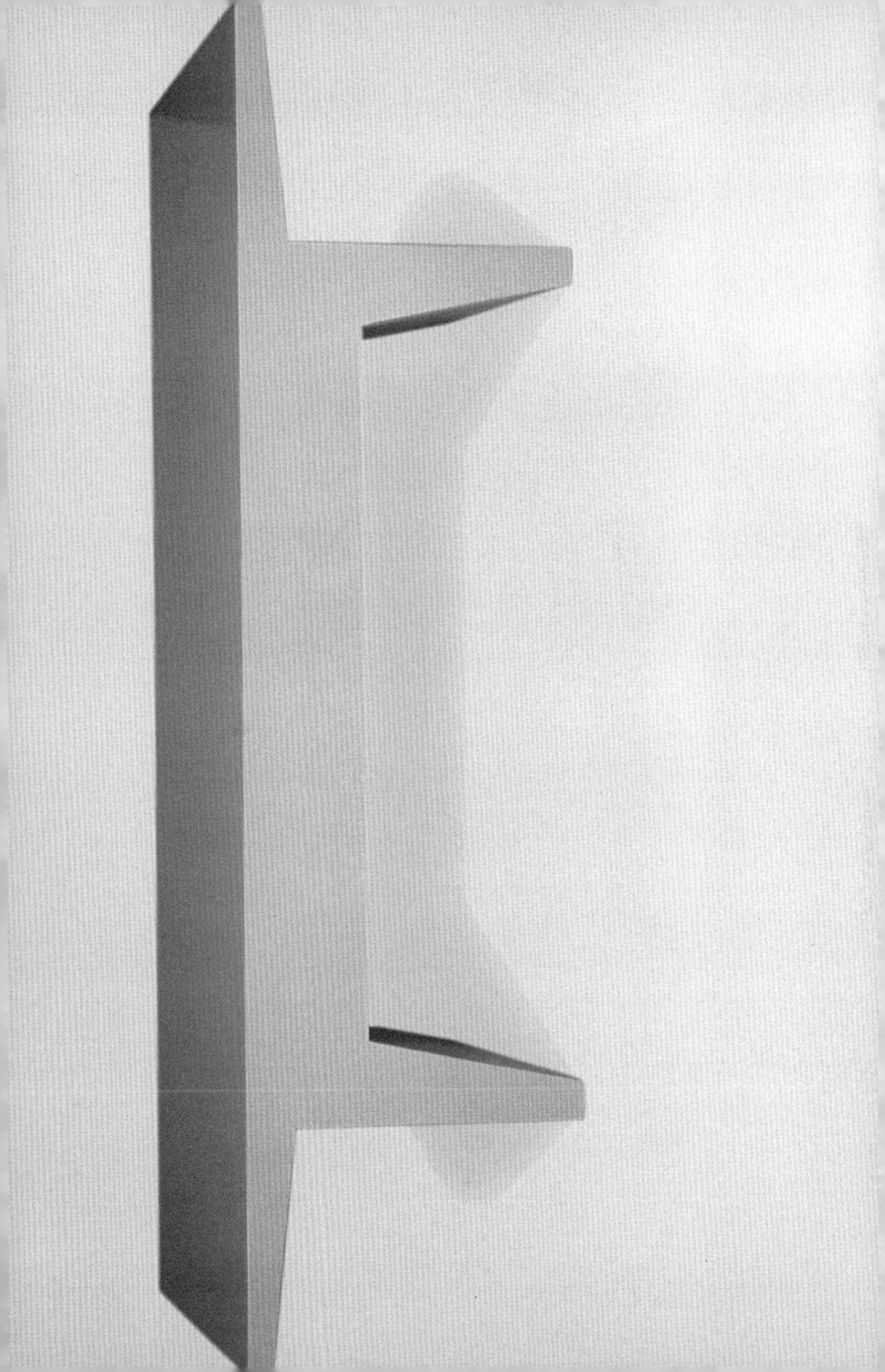

P66 凯瑟琳太太鸡尾酒台
台面凹形，可防洒溅到地面
材料：不锈钢
P66 Ms. Kathleen Cocktail Table
Top is recessed to prevent spilled beer and
toppled Pink Ladies from soiling floor.
Materials: Stainless steel

P67 FELIX 凳子
材料：MDF、漆
P67 Felix the Bench
Materials: MDF, lacquer. Available in other colors.

P68-69 托尔椅子样板
材料：橡木、胡桃木
P68-69 Thor Chair
Materials: Solid oak with walnut stain.

P70-71 HOWLA BOWLA 台，1998-2000
材料：聚酯树脂
P70-71 Howla bowla tables, 1998-2000
Materials: Cast polyester resin. Available with a
table or a bowl top. Available in other colors

P73 公爵餐桌，2000
材料：胡桃木
P73 Duke dining table, 2000
Materials: solid walnut

P74-75 4-PAC 和 6-PAC 土耳其凳
材料：不锈钢、塑料板
P74-75 4-PAC and 6-PAC Ottoman
Materials: Stainless steel, self-skinning
urethane, plastic laminate

P76 沙发
材料：不锈钢、汽车座椅塑料、高密度泡沫
P76 Lowrider Sofa, Designer: David Khouri
Materials: Stainless steel, automobile
upholstery vinyl, high density foam.

P66/P68-73/P76 设计：大卫·库力
P66/P68-73/P76 Design: David Khouri

P67/P74-75 设计：罗伯托·古兹曼
P67/P74-75 Design: Roberto Guzman

克里斯托弗·迪姆／CCD 设计公司

建筑与家具

"以简单的形式、简洁的线条与精致的细节显示阿瓦·阿尔托、雷与查里斯·埃姆斯及皮勒·肖奴的设计，迪姆精巧的设计看来是一种持久的典雅。" 提沙·索特在《美丽家居》一九九五年五月刊说道。

克里斯托弗的家具设计融合了欧洲和美国传统设计的简洁与实用。他是在米兰接受训练的建筑师，分别在孟斐斯的马提奥与安东尼奥·史特尼奥设计室接受训练。迪姆曾和美国著名建筑师弗朗克·奥·格里一起合作过。

一九九一年随着他的建筑与家具设计工作室（CCD 设计公司）的开设，迪姆反复强调美国设计在国际市场上的实力。他如今三十七岁了，其作品被国际刊物所介绍。他设计的多层架子被选入《TEN BEST》，并获得一九九九年乔治·尼尔逊奖。一九九七年最佳家具编辑奖及一九九八年国际现代家具博览会的最佳 "整体作品" 奖。在《ID》杂志一九九八年年鉴设计竞赛中获家具设计荣誉提名，并被《大都会家居》授予 "二十一世纪二十一位新人" 之一，其作品在由德国布莱曼菲力普·史达克主办的 "DESIGN MIT ZUKUNFT设计" 及在旧金山现代艺术博物馆举办的 "EAMES AND BEYOND" 展览中展出。他的作品被旧金山现代艺术博物馆所收藏，部分作品被一些收藏者和设计师收藏。

迪姆的追求是要使他的家具具有 "本质性"，在 "JIG 镜子" 的设计中体现了他的 "小即多" 的概念。"JIG 镜子" 是一块简单的弯曲胶合板，其形状适合于不同用途。"我用我称之为减少细节的方式，即细节就是要去掉的部分（如把手的孔），以达到具有个性与简洁的目的。"

以敏锐的眼光关注我们的生活或者说能够生存的方式，迪姆的作品为现代家居和办公室所需的灵活性与机动性提供了幽雅的方案。他的 BELLY 桌子不但是餐桌，还是储藏柜。"我们的家具用途极少是单一的，我尽量给用者提供自然及有创意的家具。"

克里斯托弗的家具体现一流的工艺，对材料的敏感并适应新世纪设计的清晰功能。迪姆居住在旧金山，他合理地把时间安排于自己的设计工作室、教学及冲浪运动。他说：我的工作是使我们可简单地生活，而不是对设计的痴迷。

CHRISTOPHER C. DEAM/CCD

Architecture / Furniture

"With the simplicity, clean lines, and beautiful detailing that recall the designs of Alvar Aalto, Ray and Charles Eames, and Pierre Chareau, Deam's ingenious pieces look set to become enduring classics". Tessa Souter, House Beautiful, May 1995

Christopher C. Deam's furniture blends seamlessly the simplicity and functionality of both the European and American design traditions. A Milan trained Architect who cut his teeth in the studios of both Memphis's Matteo Thun and Antonio Citterio, Deam has also worked with noted American architect Frank O. Gehry.

With the opening of CCD, his architecture and furniture design studio in 1991, he has reiterated the strength of American design in the world Market. Now thirty-seven, Deam's work has been published internationally with accolades of "Ten Best" for his tier shelves, was given the 1999 George Nelson Award, the Editor's Awards for Best Furniture in 1997 and Best Body Of Work in 1998 at the ICFF, earned honorable mention for furniture design in I.D. Magazine's 1998 annual design review, was named one of 21 rising stars for the 21st century by Metropolitan Home, and has shown extensively including the exhibitions "Design Mit Zukunft" curated by Philippe Starck in Bremen, Germany and "Eames and Beyond" at the SFMOMA. His "gallery pair" is part of the permanent collection of the San Francisco Museum of Modern Art, and his pieces are sought avidly by collectors and designers.

Deam's quest to make his furniture "essential" is epitomized in his minimal yet multifunctional design of the Jig Mirror , a simple piece of curved plywood who's shape allows for varied uses. "I use what I call reductive detailing, that is, the detail lies in what is stripped away (e.g. a hole for a handle) to give a piece its identity and attain clarity of intent."

With a keen eye focused on the way in which we live, or could live, Deam's work gives elegant solutions for the demands of flexibility and mobility required in the modern home and office. His Belly Table not only has a double sided dining surface but provides room for storage. "Very seldom do we have singular uses for things. I try to allow for spontaneity and inventiveness on the part of the user."

Christopher C. Deam's furniture embodies the superior craft, material sensitivity, and legible function pertinent to responsible design for the next century. Mr. Deam resides in San Francisco, California where he balances his time between his design studio, teaching at CCAC and U. C. Berkeley, and surfing. He says: my work is about allowing us to live simply, not an infatuation with design.

P80 艺廊柜. 1999
材料: 槭木、铝
P80 Gallery Pair Cabinet, 1999
Materials: maple ply, aluminum

P82-83 SPC 系列. 1999
材料: 泡沫
P82-83 SPV series, 1999
Materials: expanded foam

P84-85 JIP 镜子. 1999
材料: 槭木
P84-85 Jig Mirror, 1999
Materials: maple ply

P86 轻型手提电脑盒 〔样板〕
P86 lightweight laptop computer carrier (prototype)

P80/P82-86 设计: 克里斯托弗·迪姆
P80/P82-86 Design: Christopher Deam

尼克·戴恩 / 迪纳森设计公司

尼克·戴恩三十五岁，土生土长的纽约人，是著名流行艺术家吉姆·戴恩的儿子。尼克最近经营自己的室内建筑与产品设计公司－迪纳森设计公司，从建筑的翻新到陶器，其设计涵盖方方面面。

尼克·戴恩于一九八七年获得了罗得岛设计学院学士学位。在 APEX 技术学院学习了一年后，他在皇家艺术学院继续其学业并于一九九一年毕业。其后在伦敦的东区承接家具设计，协办在荷兰与苏格兰举办的英国现代设计展，戴恩的设计也在欧洲的各种家具展中展出。

自一九九三年回纽约后，戴恩就从事大量的各种规模的商业与家居室内设计。在过去六年他作为设计师、项目经理及施工协调人，所从事的项目几乎都是建筑范围内。最近的项目包括 KIRNA ZABETE，一间在纽约苏豪区的大型女性时装精品店，还有几个纽约的住宅项目。

在一九九七年纽约国际现代家具博览会中，尼克·戴恩展出了自己的家具系列—格玛储物柜系列。直到那时，戴恩主要设计订做木家具、陶瓷烟灰缸及花瓶系列。

一九九八与一九九九年的家具系列从原来的格玛储物柜发展到最近推出的几种运用工业金属生产技术制作的家庭储物产品。同时推出的还有沙发与凳子，这些产品使其设计趋于完美，在工业金属的运用上添加了柔软的特性。

最近，在纽约举办的一九九九年国际现代家具博览会上，尼克参加"G7"联合展。他的设计也在博览会中的"维逊艺术／室内设计"展位中展出，其中包括他设计的夹板与家具。"维逊艺术／室内设计"展位获得了优秀整体设计编辑奖。

尼克·戴恩的作品已被美国及世界性刊物广泛介绍，最近刊登在《ABITARE》、《大都会家居》、美国《ELLE 装饰》、意大利《ELLE 装饰》及《纽约》杂志上。

Nick Dine / DINERSAN

Nick Dine is a 35-year old New York City native, son of famous Pop artist Jim Dine, who currently runs his own interior architecture and product design firm; Dinersan, inc. From building renovations to ceramics, Dine's work covers a myriad of scales and sensibilities.

Nick Dine received his undergraduate degree from Rhode Island School of Design in 1987. After a year at Apex Technical School, he continued on to the Royal College of Art, graduating in 1991. He set up practice in London's East End, working on furniture commissions and co-curating shows of British contemporary design in Holland and Scotland. Dine also showed at various furniture fairs throughout Europe.

Since returning to New York in 1993, Dine has worked on numerous large and small scale commercial and residential interior spaces. These projects have kept Dine in the architectural realm almost exclusively for the past six years, working as designer as well as project manager and construction coordinator. Current projects include Kirna Zabete, an upscale women's fashion boutique in New York's Soho, as well as several residences around New York.

At the 1997 International Contemporary Furniture Fair in New York, Nick Dine launched his own line of custom and production furniture, the Gomer storage line. Until that time, Dine worked primarily on custom wood furniture, and a line of ceramic ashtrays and vases. The 1998-99 furniture lines grew from the original Gomer storage cabinets to several recently launched home storage products which utilize the technology of industrial metal fabrication. Launched at the same time were the upholstered sofa and bench, which rounded out the collection, lending a soft edge to compliment the industrial metal.

Recently Nick took part in the "G7" group show in New York, held during the 1999 International Contemporary Furniture Fair. He also showed work as part of the Wilsonart/Inside Design booth, within the Fair, which included both his custom designed laminate and furniture. The Wilsonart/Inside Design booth received the Editor's Award for Best Body of Work.

Nick Dine has been published extensively throughout the United States and the world, most recently in Abitare, Metropolitan Home, American Elle Decor, Italian Elle Decor, and New York Magazine.

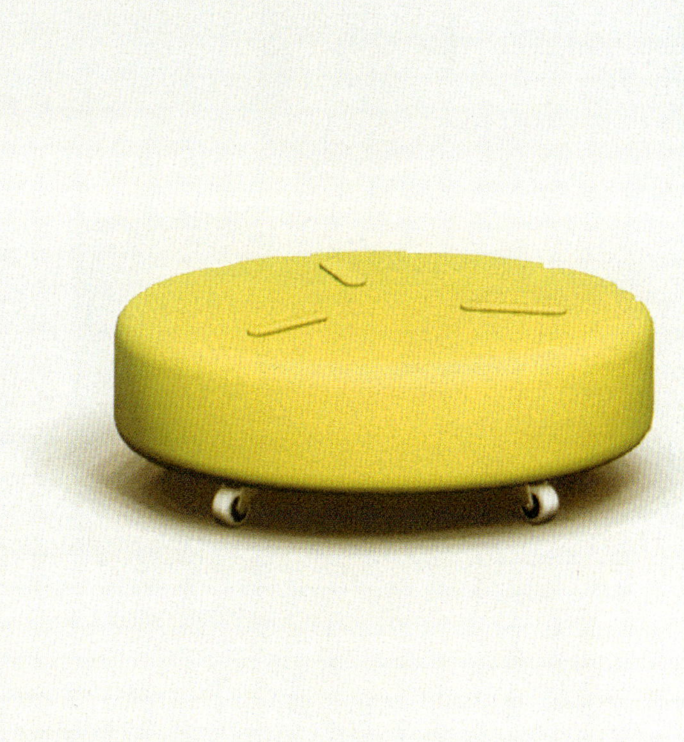

P90 书车，1998
材料：钢板
P90 Bookcart, 1998
Materials: powder coated steel

P92-93 格玛储物柜系列，1998
材料：钢板
P92-93 Gomer pile, 1998
Materials: powder coated steel

P94-95 凳子，1999
材料：氯丁橡胶
P94-95 stool, 1999
Materials: neoprene upholstery

P96-97 墙架，1999
材料：钢板
P96-97 Wall Shelves, 1999
Materials: powder coated steel

P98 柜子，2000
材料：铝、胡桃木
P98 Cyborg, 2000
Materials: side board built with solid anodized aluminum with walnut
covered wood drawers and doors, which open with touch latches.

P90/P92-98 设计：尼克·戴恩
P90/P92-98 Design: Nick Dine

恩斯组合

恩斯组合是由玛利·莫尔里，卡米拉·维加与哈利·鲍尔·凡·伊尔塞组成的设计公司。他们的合作关系始于一九九九在米兰举办的一个设计展（产品、家具、灯具及纺织品展）。

从此他们就继续合作，其合作已延伸到信息概念的交流及展览。

他们一起生产雕塑品、地毯、纺织品及其它设计品（如为艾勒斯公司做的设计），这些设计融合了材料的应用。把不同的材料—从精细的古典陶器或皮革到塑胶、塑料及 MDF 融合一起，玛利·莫尔里、哈利与卡米拉推出了有关表面材料、规格、色彩与椅垫的灵活组合，倾向于光滑的表面与简洁的形状。他们的设计基本着重于解决不同的硬材料与柔软形状结合的问题。采用再现的生态主题与不规则的生物形状，传送一种幽雅安逸的感觉。

Once Group

Once is a collaboration between Marre Moerel, Camila Vega, and Harry Paul van Iersel (Harry & Camilla). Their partnership was originally formed to facilitate an exhibition of design prototypes (product, furniture, lighting, and textiles) in an off-site gallery space during the 1999 Salone di Mobile in Milan.

They continued to work together, and their partnership has developed into an important platform for intercontinental exchange of information, contacts, ideas, and exhibitions.

Together they produce sculptural objects, carpets, textiles, and other design objects (for companies like Alessi) that all integrate a high level of material exploration. Fusing disparate materials, from fine classic earthenware or leather to plastic, vinyl to MDF, Marre Moerel & Harry & Camila propose a flexible palette of finishes, sizes, colors and upholstery, always preferring smooth surfaces and clean shapes. Their work essentially focuses in resolving the tension between various hard materials and soft shapes, conveying a sense of elegant comfort, while using recurring biological themes and forms of amorphous organisms.

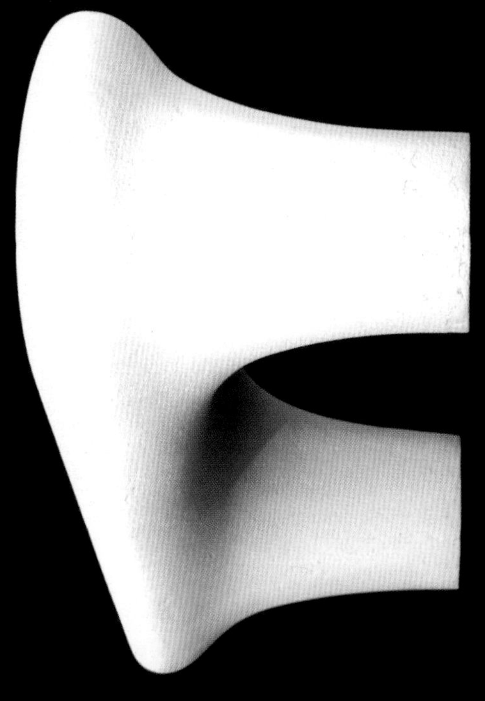

table-lighter, alessi

P104-105 软盒系列，1994
材料：陶瓷、瓷灯架、灯座、白炽灯泡
P104-105 Soft Box series, 1994
Materials: earthenware ceramic, medium
porcelain lamp holder and base, incandescent
lamp bulb

P106-107 SOFT CELL 灯具系列．1999-2000
材料：胶合板、聚乙烯塑料、普拉克斯玻璃、
白炽灯
P106-107 Soft Cell series (various series), 1999-
2000
Materials: plywood, vinyl, plexiglass, incandescent lighting.

P108 吊灯．2000
材料：陶瓷、白炽灯
P108 Polyp hanging/standing lamp, 2000
Materials: earthenware ceramic, incandescent
lighting

P109 "延伸"柜，1998
组合储物柜，用于放置软物品，如内衣裤、
玩具．表面可用不同的材料及色彩（聚乙稀
塑料、石膏板、胶合板）
材料：喷漆 MDF
P109 Grow, 1998 (prototype)
Modular storage units for soft items, such as
underwear, toys. in various finishes and colors
(vinyl, chalkboard paint, plywood)
Materials: Painted MDF

P110-111 摇摆凳、塑料凳，1998
摇摆凳以胶合板制作．椅垫以牛皮制作。凳
子采用不同的表面材料，如粗帆布．BAZE 纤
维，以毯了包起沿边缘缠合。塑料凳是以胶
合板如聚乙稀塑料组成，有不同的形状、规
格与椅垫。

P110-111 Gem, Gerrit, Cow stools, various
sizes, 1998
Cow is a rocking stool made in laminated
plywood, upholstered with cow hide and
leather. The stool comes in different finishes,
raw canvas, baze fabric, with blanket stitching,
along all edges, Gem is an upholstered stool
with a plywood structure and vinyl. Available
in different shapes, sizes, and upholstery.

P112 K'S 椅子．1999
P112 K's chair, 1999

P113 SCHAAL 椅子．1999
P113 Schaal Chair, 1999

P114 SCHAAL 椅样板．1999
P114 Schaal Chair (prototype), 1999

P115 大椅子．2000
P115 Big Seat Chair, 2000

P116-117 大椅子．1999
材料：椅垫
P116-117 Big Seat Chair, 1999
Materials: upholstery

P104-111 设计：玛利·莫尔里
P104-111 Design: Marre Moerel

P112-117 设计：哈利、卡米拉
P112-117 Design: Harry & Camila

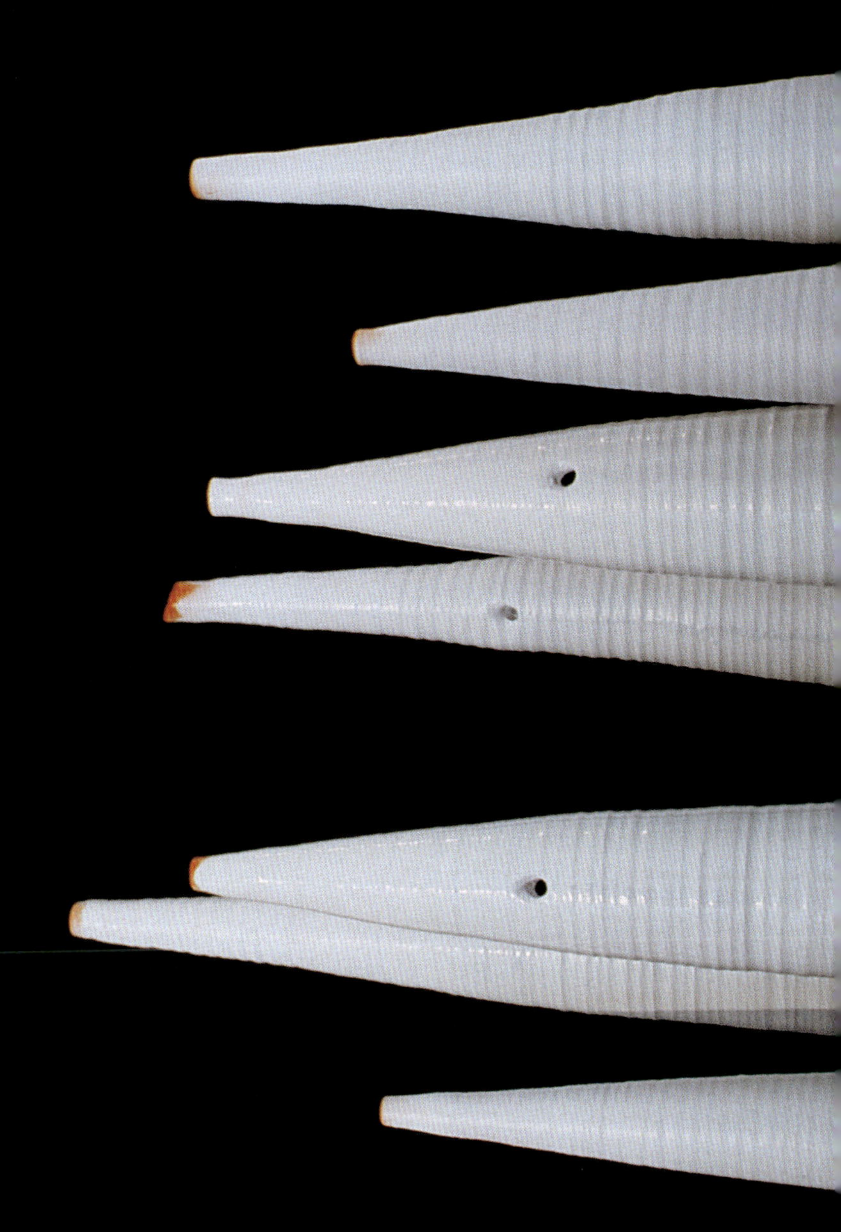

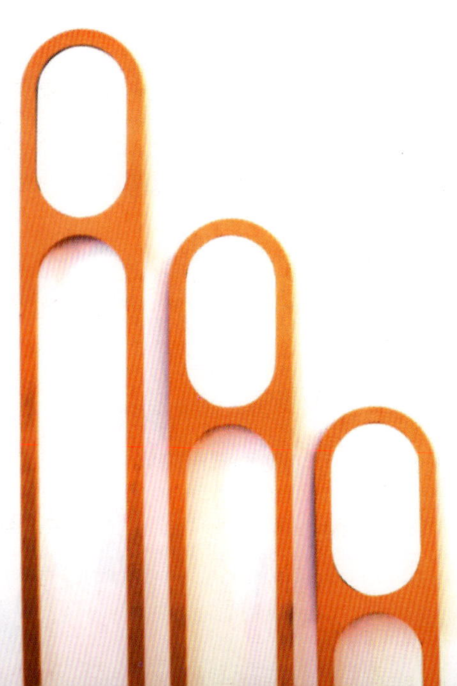

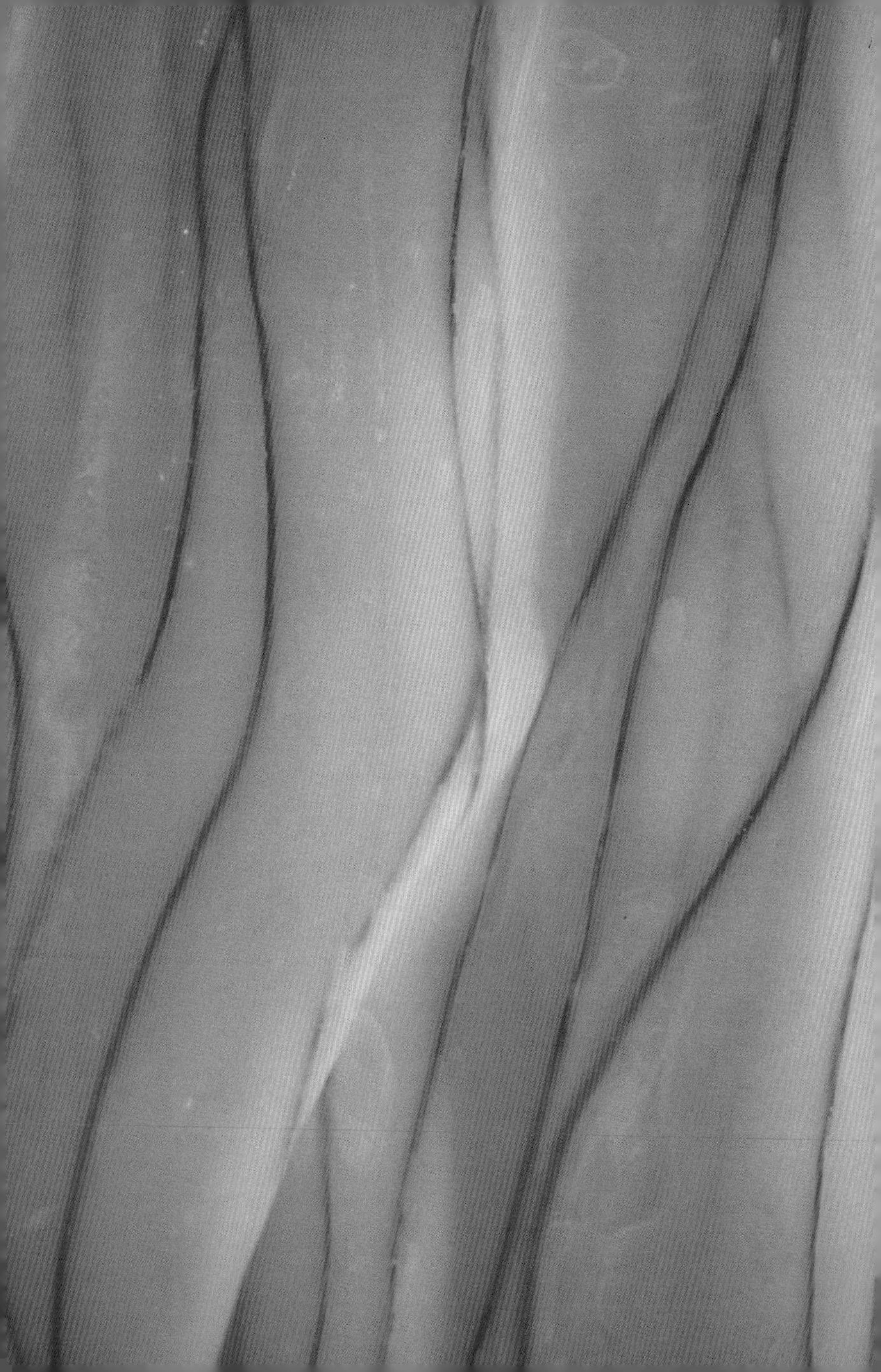

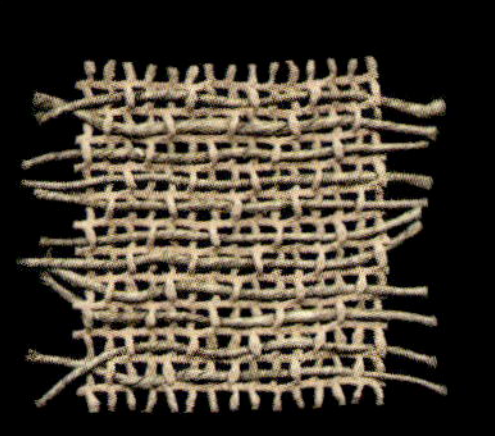

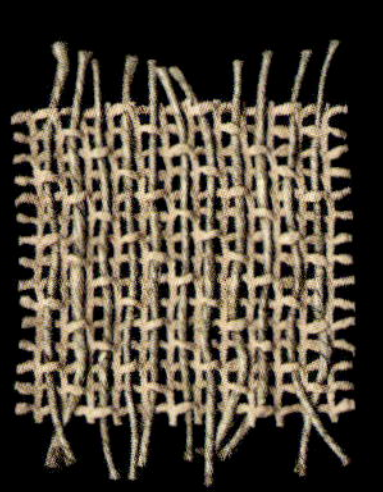

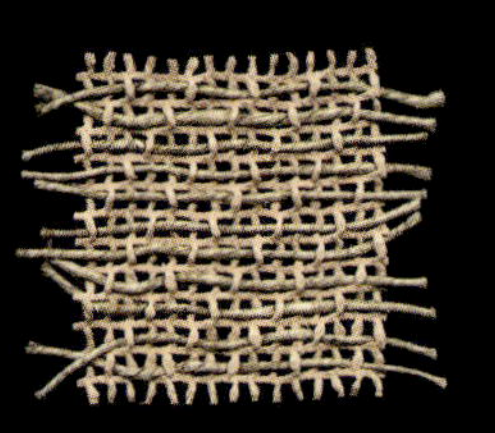

P118 CHERNO 台凳样板
材料：木、泡沫
P118 Cherno Bench Table
Materials: wood, foam

P119 墙边桌．2000
材料：普列克斯玻璃
P119 Sidetable , 2000
Materials: plexiglass

P120 艾勒斯火机．1999
P120 Gaslighter, Alessi, 1999

P122-123 藤壶砖．样板．2000
材料：陶瓷
P122-123 Barnacle Tiles (prototype), 2000
Materials: earthenware ceramic

P124 圆锥体．2000
材料：手造陶瓷
P124 Look Up Marroon Cones, 2000
Materials: hand made ceramic (cones)

P125 陶瓷花瓶
P125 Ceramic Vases

P126-127 兄弟镜．2000
材料：MDF、木、镜
P126-127 Mirrors Brothers D, 2000
Materials: MDF, wood, mirror

P128-132 桌布纹理
所有这些实验包括了硅材料、多种纤维材料。实验展示在《创新纤维趋势》书中，该书的销售对象是使用这些新纤维的汽车行业。

P128-132 Table cloth textures
All are experiments including silicone based materials, various kinds of materials woven into fabric. These experiments are shown in a book of trends of innovative fabrics that are meant to be sold to corporate companies such as the automobile industry using these new fabrics for cars, products and public transports interiors, etc.

P118-120/P124-132 设计：哈利、卡米拉
P118-120/P124-132 Design: Harry & Camila

P122-123 设计：玛利·莫尔里
P122-123 Design: Marre Moere!

罗斯·梅纽兹与克里斯·邦迪／样板制作公司

罗斯·梅纽兹与克里斯·邦迪于一九九八年创立样板制作公司。样板制作公司是一间实践性工作室，在本地设计与生产家具，弥补了一些美国家具生产的空白，即让年轻设计师可以生产设计成品。

他们提供金属、塑料、橡胶、栓皮、陶瓷及毡料。罗斯·梅纽兹设计大多数的家具，而克里斯·邦迪则在他的位于布鲁克林区的店里进行制作。自一九九九年以来，梅纽兹受伦敦的 HABITAT 公司委任，对该公司的家具系列进行拓展及艺术指导，同时，邦迪专注生产其它设计师的样板。这种二重奏的合作在一些展览及室内设计家具项目上继续。

Ross Menuez and Chris Bundy/Prototype & Production

Ross Menuez and Chris Bundy / Prototype & Production formed by Ross Menuez and Chris Bundy in 1998, Prototype & Production is a "hands-on" studio, designing and fabricating furniture locally. P & P is a typical response to the lack of an integrated American manufacturing process allowing young designers to produce design pieces. The team's approach is rendered in metal, plastic, rubber, cork, ceramic, and felt. While Ross Menuez designed most of the furniture pieces, Chris Bundy manufactured them in his shop in Brooklyn. Since 1999, Menuez has been called on by Habitat in London to develop and art direct their in-house line of furniture, meanwhile Bundy focuses on producing other designers' prototypes. The duo continues to collaborate over the Atlantic on some objects, exhibitions and built-in furniture for New York interiors.

P136 DOZCI 尼龙吊灯．1997
材料：尼龙
P136 Dozci hanging lamp in nylon, 1997
Materials: Nylon

P137 折叠尼龙莲花灯．1997
材料：折叠尼龙
P137 Anemone Lamp , 1997
Materials: folded nylon

P138-139 毡屏风．1998
材料：工业毡、不锈钢
P138-139 Felt Screen, 1998
Materials: industrial felt, stainless steel

P140-143 "标准" 酒吧室内设计．P1998-1999
"标准" 酒吧位于曼克顿东下区第一大道 159 号
P140-143 The Standard bar, 1998-1999
3 views of the interior of the Standard bar located in Lower East side of
Manhattan, 159 First Avenue.

P144 橡胶手提袋．1999
P144 Rubber Hand Bag, 1999

P136-144 设计：样板制作公司
P136-144 Design: Prototype & Production

迈克尔·索里斯／渥克斯公司（前），迪纳森设计公司（现）

迈克尔·索里斯出生于得克萨斯州达拉斯。过去十一年一直生活在纽约，其中的六年经营自己的渥克斯公司，一间产品设计公司。其后加盟尼克·戴恩的迪纳森设计公司，在该公司工作了一段时间后，他最近决定回家。

迈克尔于一九九一年获得柏森斯设计学院的硕士学位，不久便在布鲁克林丹博区设立了自己的工作室，从事家具与场景设计的项目。他在一九九五年纽约国际现代家具博览会上展出了自己的首套家具及家居用品设计。

在一九九六年的纽约国际现代家具博览会上，迈克获得了优秀新人编辑奖。他对简结线条与材料的运用已使自己归纳到为数不多的正拓展新风格的美国年轻现代设计师的行列中。最近迈克尔与其他的六位设计师开创了先例，举办他们自己的"G7"卫星联展。在一九九九年与二零零零年的国际家具博览会中，"G7"联展在纽约设计圈引起极大的反响。

从一九九九年至二零零零年，迈克尔开始与尼克·戴恩合作，加盟尼克·戴恩的迪纳森设计公司，设计与策划纽约众多的室内设计项目。同时他也在纽约市TOTEM艺廊展示其作品。欧洲与美国的多种刊物刊登了迈克尔的作品，如最近的《ABITARE》，《SURFACE》，《室内》杂志及《HARPER'S BAZAAR》杂志。

迈克尔·索里斯在科幻片里寻求灵感，并受到"星球大战"及"矩阵"电影的影响。未来主义的几何形状以及光滑材料是索里斯检朴设计的特点，这种设计看来是产生于电脑制作的形象。

Michael Solis / formerly Worx, now DINERSAN

Michael Solis was born in Dallas, Texas. He has been living in New York for the past eleven years, six of which Michael has run his own studio, WORX, a product design firm. After working with Nick Dine/Dinersan, solis recently decided to go back home. He is now currently working with Nick Dine for Dinersan, inc.

Michael received his undergraduate degree from Parsons School of Design in 1991 and started his own studio shortly thereafter in the D.U.M.B.O area of Brooklyn. There he worked on projects such as furniture and set design. In 1995, Michael launched his first line of furniture and home accessories at the International Contemporary Furniture Fair in New York.

At the 1996 I.C.F.F in New York, Michael won the Editor's Award for Best New Designer. His use of clean lines and materials has set him in the path with a small number of young contemporary designers in America who are developing a new style. Most recently, Michael and six other designers set a precedent by creating their own satellite show, "G7", during the 1999 and 2000 I.C.F.F., which created an enormous response towards new work in the field of design.

In 1999-2000 Michael began working with Nick Dine, and his company Dinersan, inc. on designing and project managing numerous interior projects in New York. He also shows work at Totem NYC. Michael has been published in various publications throughout Europe and America. Currently; Abitare, Surface, Interior magazine and Harper's Bazaar.

Michael Solis finds inspiration in science fiction, influenced by *Star Wars* and *The Matrix*. Futuristic geometric forms, with smooth material characterize Solis' spare designs which seem to have been born out of computer generated imagery.

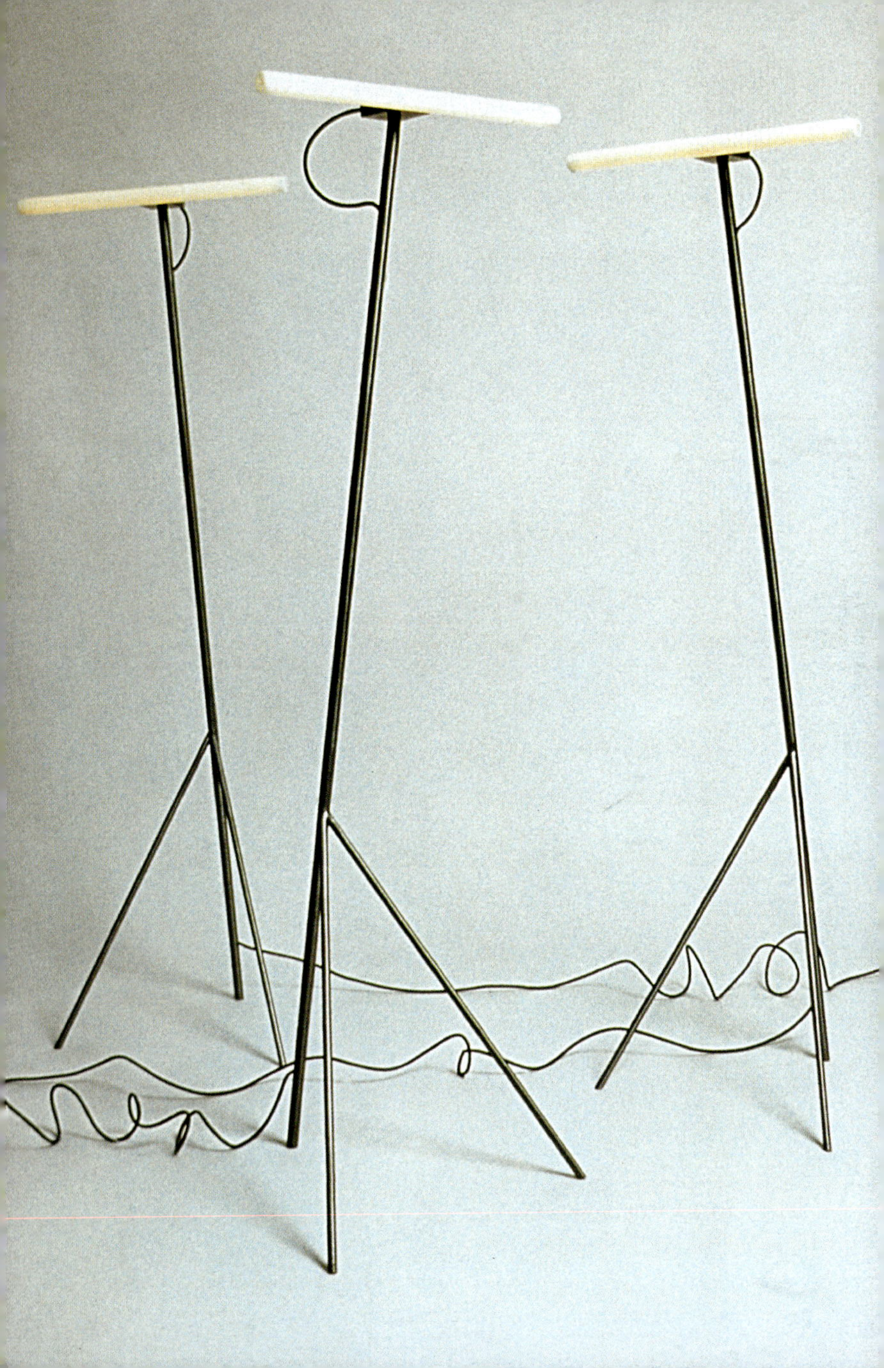

P148/P150-151 DEFENDER 凳，1999
材料：铝管、椅垫
P148/P150-151 Defender Stools, 1999
Materials: Aluminum Tubing, custom made upholstering in
ultrasuede or ultraleather

P152 花盆，1999
材料：陶瓷
P152 Land Craters/Planters, 1999
Materials: ceramic

P153 "米奥"凳，2000
材料：聚乙稀座垫、铝管
P153 "Mio" bench, 2000
Materials: vinyl dipped seat cushion, aluminum tubing

P154-155 桌子，2000
桌面附有储物架
材料：胡桃木、铝桌脚
P154 Fuse+ end table, 2000
With extra storage shelving system incorporated in the top
Materials: walnut, aluminum legs

P156-157 矮咖啡桌，2000
矮咖啡桌带有滑动抽屉的储物柜，一个柜子可装 440 只 CD 或杂志
材料：胡桃木、无白光漆板、铝桌脚
P156-157 Four Forty, 2000
A low coffee table with storage included in sliding central drawer,
allowing one to store more than 440 CDs, or magazines.
Materials: walnut, white matte painted structure board, aluminum
feet

P158 摇头地灯，1999
材料：金属管
P158 Hammerhead Floorlamps, 1999
Materials: Metal Tubing

P148-158 设计：迈克尔·索里斯
P148-158 Design: Michael Solis

〔京〕新登字 083 号

图书在版编目〔CIP〕数据

G7 组合的产品设计／王序主编．—北京：

中国青年出版社，2001

（设计新视点丛书）

ISBN 7-5006-4087-0

I．G…　II．王…　III．产品－设计－美国－图集　IV．TB472-64

中国版本图书馆 CIP 数据核字〔2000〕第 79421 号

书名：G7 组合的产品设计

主编、设计：王序

制作：王序设计有限公司

广州天河区林和中路 158 号天誉花园悠雅阁 2104-2105

邮政编码：510610　传真：020 38840350

E-mail: xu@wangxu.com.cn

责任编辑：王寒柏

出版：中国青年出版社

社址：北京东四十二条 21 号

邮政编码：100708

网址：http://www.cyp.com.cn

发行：中国青年出版社北京图书发行部

电话：010 64010813　传真：010 84027892

分色：深圳幸运电脑组版有限公司

印刷：深圳雅昌彩色印刷有限公司

经销：新华书店

开本：787 × 1092mm　1/32

印张：5

字数：10 千字

版次：2001 年 1 月北京第 1 版

印次：2001 年 1 月深圳第 1 次印刷

印数：1-5,000 册

ISBN 7-5006-4087-0/J·420

定价：50.00 元